Michael O. Amamieye

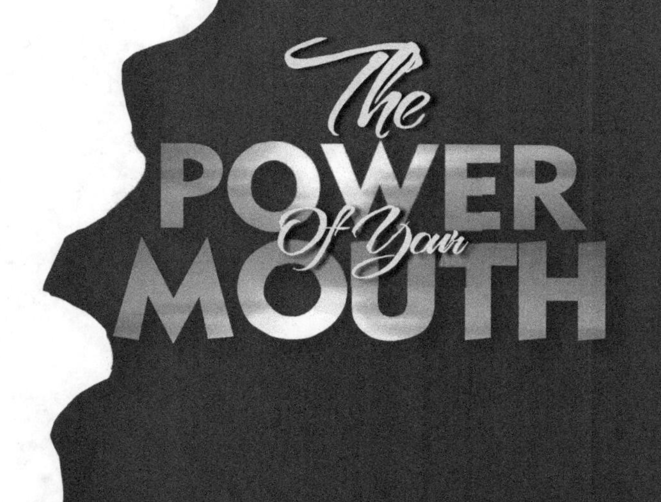

1

Published by:
**Michael Amamieye Word Outreach, International
a/k/a Aggressive Faith Ministries,
Plot 13 Walter Akpana Lay Out off 394
Ikwerre Road Mile 5 Rumueprikom
P. O. Box 12378, Port Harcourt, Nigeria.
E-mail: info@aggressivefaith.org
Web site: www.aggressivefaith.org
Phone: +234-9018006296, +2348050987377
+1-916-245-6157 (U.S.A.)
WhatsApp: +2348036732188**

ISBN: 978-35362-6-5-006

Printed in the Federal Republic of Nigeria.

DEDICATION

This book is dedicated to my covenant friends, Apostle Calvin Cook in San Jose, California; Pastor Margie Mitchell in Elyria, Ohio; Pastor Matthew Uponi in Calgary, Canada.

CONTENT

INTRODUCTION

The power of your mouth is a demonstration of what your consistent confessions of your mouth can do to literally change your life. Most people don't know how powerful they are until they see for themselves what they have spoken consistently come to pass.

Jesus shows us the example of what you say consistently will come to pass good or bad. Several times Jesus said that He was going to be killed and then He would rise again. It was a bold declaration of what His life would be. He did not live at the mercy of His killers. He said it. It happened as He said it.

"And they shall mock him, and shall scourge him, and shall spit upon him, and shall kill him: and the third day he shall rise again."

Mark 10:34.

How would you like to live like this? I know you would want to see your words work wonders. Yes, you can. He said it. It came to pass just as He said.

"And the angel answered and said unto the women, Fear not ye: for I know that ye seek Jesus, which was crucified.

He is not here: for he is risen, as he said. Come, see the place where the Lord lay."

Matt. 28:5-6.

Did you see that? The angel reported, ***He is not here: for He is risen, as He said.*** This is one power you have as well in Christ. I remember some years ago when I traveled to Haiti and Dominican Republic. Archbishop Idem Ikon and I went on that mission. My friend who coordinated that mission told us that the journey from Port au Prince to Monte Plata was not far. On the contrary, it was a long journey by bus. When we arrived at midnight, my immune system was already down. We finished our outreaches there and returned to Port au Prince where we had several outreaches and a conference before we left. The mosquitoes in Haiti really dealt with me plus the heat. The temperature that time was above forty degrees Celsius. It was tough.

At the airport, after I checked in for the flight to New York, my body caved in. I collapsed. I was practically wheeled unto the plane. One of our travel companions on that flight was a relation to the owners of the hotel we stayed. He was gracious to give me some tablets for chukunguya. On arrival at New York, my face was swollen. In fact, the passport officer almost refused me entry because my actual face and that on my passport were not the same. Eventually, after back and forth conversation, his supervisor used my eye lash to identify me and I was granted entry. From there, I traveled to Newark where I was to catch my next flight to Amsterdam for another meeting. At Newark, I got my friend, Dr. Yemi Adedeji to give me some Fancida for malaria.

I boarded that flight from Newark. I was passenger seat 2A. Two hours into the flight, my whole body began to feel sick. I told the air hostess I needed pepper. I would have been alright with that. There was no pepper except for the American pepper. Before I knew it, the supervisor and the pilot took a decision to divert the plane to St. John's, Newfoundland, Canada. That was how I found myself quarantined in the St. Johns Hospital, Newfoundland. This was when Ebola was making the news. When the Chief Medical Director came to see me, he said, you are sick. I told him, I am not sick. Then, he said, you brought a whole plane down, you are sick. I told him, I am not sick. He said it the third time, you are sick. For the third time, I told him, I am not sick. For three days, they did all manner of test and checks. At the end of all the test and checks, the result was a clean bill of health because when he said, you are sick, I told him, I am not sick. My confession cancelled even malaria that is in every Nigerian blood. The entire test for Ebola, HIV and AIDS, malaria, etc, came out negative. There is power in your mouth to change your present condition.

Chapter One
THE POWER OF YOUR MOUTH

***"If any man among you seem to be religious,
and bridleth not his tongue, but deceiveth his
own heart, this man's religion is vain."***
James 1:26.

The force or energy or power of any religion is
in the mouth. It begins with the mouth, continues
with the mouth and culminates with the mouth.
James 1:26 tells us that if anyone is trying to be
religious without his mouth, he is only deceiving
himself. In fact, his religion is vain. It is
worthless. It is powerless.

How can you say that you are a religious person
without any proof or evidence? The proof begins
with your mouth. This proof is further fired up
by your mouth as you keep speaking and
affirming the things that you believe.

Look at James 3:1-18 and you will find for yourself the tremendous power that is locked up in your mouth. With your mouth, you can literally gain the mastery of your circumstances and situations in life. You can become the master of your situation and circumstance. You don't have to leave your life to chance or fate. You can choose what happens to you. You can change what you find around you. There is tremendous power in your mouth.

"If anyone can control his tongue, it proves that he has perfect control over himself in every other way."
James 3:2. The Living Bible.

You can bridle your whole body with your mouth. Your entire physical form can be shaped and formed by your mouth. Wow! This might deliver somebody from spending too much money on cosmetics, plastic surgery and medication. Are you sick and tired of your physical form? Are you embarrassed by the size of your body? Have you been a laughing stock to your family members, friends, colleagues and comrades that you want to see a change desperately? Your change has come.

The power to change your body form is in your mouth. You can change those bad eating habits you have cultivated over the years beginning from today. You can change your size or shape from today without medication or money. This one has no side effect. And, it is for free. It is all in your mouth.

You can bridle your whole body with your mouth. You can reduplicate your whole body. That really gets me excited. It says, **your whole body.** No part of your body is exempted. Every part is subject to change by the power of your mouth. Just stand in front of your mirror and take a look at yourself. See what areas of your body that needs to be changed from today.

Write it down.

Tell yourself, this one has got to go.

This one needs to be enlarged.

This one needs to be reduced.

This one needs to stop growing.

This one needs to grow.

"Behold, we put bits in the horses' mouths, that they may obey us; and we turn about their whole body."
James 3:3.

No matter how wild a horse is, you can literally make that horse obey you and turn about its whole body. This is in comparison to what you can do to your body no matter the years of abuse you have suffered. Your body may have been used to a certain way because of age, habit, hurts and hang ups. But you can make it to obey you.

You can turn it about. You can convince your body to follow another pattern of living. It is like this now because many days or weeks or months ago, you convinced it to live like this. Now, change it by convincing it to live differently. By convincing it, you can lead it in the direction of your conviction.

If it takes just a bit in the mouth of a wild horse to subject it, all it will require is your mouth to change your body to become what you want it to become from today. It does not take much to change. It takes just a little bit. That little bit is your mouth. Your life can change if you put your mouth to work in the direction of your change.

"Behold also the ships, which though they be so great, and are driven of fierce winds, yet are they turned about with a very small helm, whithersoever the governor listeth."
James 3:4.

As great as ships are, even when driven by fierce winds, it only requires a small helm to make it go where you want it to go. That implies that no matter how big your body is, you can change it. No matter how big your situation is, you can change it. No matter the damage that has been done to you in life, you can change it. What looks impossible is possible.

"Even so the tongue is a little member, and boasteth great things. Behold, how great a matter a little fire kindleth!
And the tongue is a fire, a world of iniquity: so is the tongue among our members, that it defileth the whole body, and setteth on fire the course of nature; and it is set on fire of hell."
James 3:5-6.

Look at how little your tongue is compared to the size of your body. No wonder we have despised it over the years. It is so little that you can easily ignore and underestimate it. But this moment, by this book, I am bringing to your knowledge the inherent power in your tongue. There is tremendous power in your tongue.

Just take a look at what the little member in your body can do. It boasts about great things. It can lay claim to great things that the hands are yet to handle. Every time you look at your big house and you tell people, that is my house. You can't carry it along with you but your tongue has hold of it. Even when it is in dispute, your tongue has claim on it. It is so little but mighty. It is so little but dynamic.

Greatness is really not in size but in strength. It will always take the lesser light to rule the night. Gen. 1:16. Your tongue can literally cause great things to happen to you.

What are those great things in your heart that you want to see come to pass?

Write them down on a separate sheet of paper.

Look at them closely.

Your tongue as little as it is can make them come to pass in your lifetime.

The scripture went further to tell us that the tongue is a fire. It can set the course of nature on fire. The fire that has gone out of your life can be restored by your tongue. The fire that has gone out of your relationship can be restored by the power of your tongue.

When you hear someone say that the love they have for their spouse is gone, it is because they said so. If you want it back, speak it with your mouth. When you tell someone that you have lost faith or confidence in them or the system, it is because you said so. If you want it back, speak it with your mouth.

Are you not surprised that the person you said is not trust-worthy is highly esteemed by some others? When you said that they are not trust worthy, it is because you said it. Now, change it with your mouth.

Everybody needs fire in their lives.

Fire is energy.

Fire is enthusiasm.

Fire is enveloping.

Fire can catch attention like it caught the attention of Moses.

"Now Moses kept the flock of Jethro his father in law, the priest of Midian: and he led the flock to the backside of the desert, and came to the mountain of God, even to Horeb.
And the angel of the Lord appeared unto him in a flame of fire out of the midst of a bush: and he looked, and, behold, the bush burned with fire, and the bush was not consumed.
And Moses said, I will now turn aside, and see this great sight, why the bush is not burnt.
And when the Lord saw that he turned aside to see, God called unto him out of the midst of the bush, and said, Moses, Moses. And he said, Here am I."
Exodus 3:1-4.

Have you been waiting and praying for someone to love you and really express it to you? Have you desired to get into fruitful relationships that will change your status? Do you desire a partner in life, marriage or ministry? You need fire that will attract them to you. Get ready because in a short while from now, you will rejoice. Receive that fire that will cause you to become an attraction in Jesus name. Amen.

*"For every kind of beasts, and of birds, and of serpents, and of things in the sea, is tamed, and hath been tamed of mankind:
But the tongue can no man tame; it is an unruly evil, full of deadly poison."*
James 3:7-8.

This is how to harness the power of the tongue by taming it. If you can tame your tongue, you can control your life. If you can tame your tongue, you can bridle your whole body. If you can tame your tongue, you can free yourself of every poison in your life.

The tongue has deadly poisons because of the fallen state of man. **DEADLY POISONS.** Poisons that bring death. Poisons that deaden your capacity, capability and creativity. Now take a look at your life, see some of those deadly poisons you put on yourself. It came from your mouth.

Many have died prematurely because they killed themselves by poisoning their lives with some of the poisons in their tongue.

Poisons in your body.

Poisons in your marriage.

Poisons in your relationships.

Poisons in your business.

Poisons in your office.

Where did they come from?

Look at your mirror and see where they came from: your mouth. I know of adults who stopped growing many years ago because of some deadly poisons that a parent or teacher or loved one placed on them. Poisons that were splashed over your life from the verbal abuses of people you looked up to and adored. The people that told you that you would never amount to anything in life. You sucked in all that poison but your change has come.

If you can tame or train your tongue, your life will be better. Now I want to ask you to make a quality decision to use your tongue properly from today. Tell yourself and speak it out loud: **From today, I decide to use my tongue to bless my life. I decide to use my tongue to bless my world. I will not poison my life again with my tongue.**

Your tongue was trained to curse and swear. Now, retrain your tongue to bless. Anytime a negative or curse or swear word wants to come out, just catch your mouth. Be deliberate about it. Instead of the negative word, speak the positive one. Instead of the curse word, speak the blessing. It will take you time and practice to perfect speaking the right words to yourself.

"Therewith bless we God, even the Father; and therewith curse we men, which are made after the similitude of God.

Out of the same mouth proceedeth blessing and cursing. My brethren, these things ought not so to be."
James 3:9-10.

Out of your mouth comes forth both blessing and cursing. You can settle for anyone of the above. You can choose to bless your world. To bless means to speak well of. You can also choose to curse your world. To curse means to speak ill or evil of and upon. You choose your choice. You choose your pick. Decide what you want.

"Doth a fountain send forth at the same place sweet water and bitter?
Can the fig tree, my brethren, bear olive berries? either a vine, figs? so can no fountain both yield salt water and fresh.
Who is a wise man and endued with knowledge among you? let him shew out of a good conversation his works with meekness of wisdom." James 3:11-13.

There is a twist to all of this in James 3:11 to 13. These verses show that what comes out of your mouth is the result of what you have been endued with. It is dependent on the knowledge you have acquired over the years. If you take care of the root, the fruit will be okay. The root really is what determines the fruit. The fruit is what people see. The root is not seen most times.

Let us look at the root of your life. What have you been feeding on? It will show if it is good or bad. What have you been listening to? It will show if it is good or bad. Who has been your motivation? It will show if they are good or bad. You can see that you can literally take charge of your world from today. This change will begin from the things you feed your eyes, ears and heart with. This change will begin when you change the company of people you listen to.

"Don't be fooled by those who say such things. If you listen to them you will start acting like them."
1 Cor. 15:33. The Living Bible.

Chapter Two
PROGRAM FOR CHANGE

I have seen that for you to be in shape, you need a program that is just good for you as a person. You cannot use another person's program to achieve your goals. There is an exercise program for pregnant woman that is not necessarily for everyone. There is an exercise program you get into that can harm you instead of helping you. What you need is the right packaging just for you.

This is very important so you don't injure yourself. I remember some years ago, I was passing through Paris. I stayed at a hotel at the airport. The next morning, I went to use the gym. I had worked for about fifteen minutes and was tired. I should have left but I saw some Asians who were exercising like they were preparing for the Olympics. My own exercise is just to stay in shape and not for any competition with anyone or group. For whatever reason, something told me that if I left after just fifteen minutes, those Asians would look at me and think that I am lazy. So I kept pushing myself until I injured myself. It took me several weeks to recover from that injury. After that day, I told myself that I will never compete with Olympic champions in exercise unless that is what I want to do. That is why you have to know the program that fits you.

A program is a package or plan of action with a set of related measures or activities in order to achieve a long term goal. It can also be a sheet or booklet detailing items to be performed in an event.

My wife is into health and fitness. She helps people live younger longer. She has a program for every one of her clients. Each program helps each client to achieve their goal. No two people should use the same program because what is good for one may not be good for another. However, there is a general template or framework every program is built. So let us build your own program from the master template.

For this program, we will begin with your heart because that is where it all begins. If you have not yet had a heart transplant, you are about to. This is important because all the problems of human life begin at the heart. That is the center of life. I remember preaching at Auchi in Edo State of Nigeria where a woman had her legs all swollen. She was told by the doctors that she had a heart defect. At one point, I mentioned by word of knowledge that someone was healed of a heart situation. This woman received it. She went home, slept and woke up the next morning to a surprise package. Her swollen legs had become normal. Someone could spend money and time treating the swollen legs and never get any result.

Until the root is taken care of, the fruit will never change.

The miracle happened when her heart was healed. Many lives are battered today because of broken hearts. Today, let us mend your broken heart by so doing we will begin the process of mending your broken life.

"And God saw that the wickedness of man was great in the earth, and that every imagination of the thoughts of his heart was only evil continually."
Gen. 6:5.

Change begins in the heart. You need a heart transplant.

**"Thus saith the Lord; Cursed be the man that trusteth in man, and maketh flesh his arm, and whose heart departeth from the Lord.
For he shall be like the heath in the desert, and shall not see when good cometh; but shall inhabit the parched places in the wilderness, in a salt land and not inhabited.
Blessed is the man that trusteth in the Lord, and whose hope the Lord is.**

*For he shall be as a tree planted by the waters,
and that spreadeth out her roots by the river,
and shall not see when heat cometh, but her
leaf shall be green; and shall not be careful in
the year of drought, neither shall cease from
yielding fruit.
The heart is deceitful above all things, and
desperately wicked: who can know it?
I the Lord search the heart, I try the reins, even
to give every man according to his ways, and
according to the fruit of his doings."*
Jeremiah 17:5-10.

The scripture above shows us the state of every heart that has departed from God and the fruits they manifest. The heart that has departed from God is deceitful and desperately wicked. It is deceiving and deceitful. It is desperate.

These are the three characteristics of the human heart until it is regenerated:

Deceitful – full of deceit.

Deceiving – can deceive and deceived.

Desperate – can be desperate to do anything for any reason.

Are you been deceived by people?

Are you desperate to get married?

Hold it right there. It is all in your heart. It shows the true condition of your heart. Your heart is evil. You need a change.

A deceitful and desperate heart will produce curses in your mouth. This eventually plants you in the desert where you will not see good but evil events and happenings around your life. When your heart is cleaned out and changed, your tongue will produce blessings. These blessings will position you in a place where you will not see evil any more. Your leaf shall be green. You will be beautiful without make up. You will look good without you making the effort to impress someone.

Two things you need for a change of heart: you need to ask Jesus Christ to come into your heart by faith.

"That Christ may dwell in your heart by faith; that ye, being rooted and grounded in love."
Eph. 3:17.

When Christ comes into your heart, He roots out every evil roots out of your life. He grounds you in His love so that love will begin to manifest in your world. How do you accept Jesus Christ into your heart? It is by faith. You believe that He is real. He came to this world. He suffered for your sins. He died on the cross for you. He was buried and on the third day, He rose from the dead. He is alive today and He is knocking on the door of your heart. Are you ready to let Him in this moment?

If you are ready, say this prayer out loud: **Jesus, I believe that you were born of a virgin. You walked this earth. You suffered for me. You died for me. I sinned and deserved to die but You took my place. You paid the price for my**

redemption. Jesus, I believe. Come into my heart now and be the Lord and Master of my life from this moment. Jesus, You are alive in me. You are real in me. Thank you for saving me today in Jesus name. Amen.

If you prayed that prayer, Jesus has entered your heart and your change has begun. You don't have to feel anything. It is all by faith.

The next thing you need to do as part of this program is to feed your mind with the knowledge of God's word. You need to be endued with knowledge. James 3:13. Get yourself a Bible that you can read daily. Begin reading it from Ephesians. As you read, mark every where it tells you who you are, what you are and what you have in Christ. Meditate on them. Dwell on them for long.

Invest on good books that will help you in this direction. Buy tapes of messages that will bless your life. Read and listen to messages on a regular basis. Fill and flood your life with messages. At this beginning point you may look abnormal to many. Don't let that bother you. Where you are going is more important than their opinion of you. They may ridicule you now but tomorrow they will respect you.

"And be not conformed to this world: but be ye transformed by the renewing of your mind, that ye may prove what is that good, and acceptable, and perfect, will of God."
Rom. 12:2.

Renew or retrain your mind to think in the direction of where you want your life to go. This means you will discipline yourself to listen to only those who will inspire and help you to get to your destination. You will discipline yourself to hearing what God has to say in spite of popular opinion.

"And He said to them, Be careful what you are hearing. The measure [of thought and study] you give [to the truth you hear] will be the measure [of virtue and knowledge] that comes back to you-and more [besides] will be given to you who hear."

Mark 4:24. Amplified Version.

When you hear a good message, buy the tape. If you have to miss a meal or more, do it. You will not die. What you cannot afford today, by tomorrow when your life will be in good shape you can afford it several times over. Write to me today and request for messages that will help you in any area of your life. I will make sure that you get the specific message that will help your life to become better.

Chapter Three
PRESCRIPTION FOR CHANGE

Each time you go to the doctor for a situation, there is diagnosis and a prescription. A diagnosis identifies the nature of an illness or any other problem identified by examination using the symptoms described by the patient. From the diagnosis, the doctor prescribes a treatment plan or schedule which must be religiously followed by the patient if they must achieve their goal of wellness. This prescription is a written instruction for treatment.

God's word has a prescription for your change in life. It contains specific instructions which you must follow if you really desire to see changes in your life and world.

"My son, attend to my words; incline thine ear unto my sayings.

*Let them not depart from thine eyes; keep them
in the midst of thine heart.
For they are life unto those that find them, and
health to all their flesh .
Keep thy heart with all diligence; for out of it
are the issues of life.
Put away from thee a froward mouth, and
perverse lips put far from thee.
Let thine eyes look right on, and let thine
eyelids look straight before thee."*
Prov. 4:20-25.

Your ears, eyes and mouth will play a major role in your recovery process. What you feed your eyes, ears and mouth with will determine whether you will achieve your goal of a changed life or not. These are the three gateways to your heart. Anything that goes through your eyes, ears and mouth will affect what goes on in your heart. What goes on in your heart will eventually affect every aspect of your life and world.

Do you really want to see dramatic changes in your body?

Do you want to see dramatic changes in your relationships?

Do you want to be well, happy and blessed?

Then, you must begin this program that will change your life forever. Do these things daily:

One, pay attention to what God is saying to you. Give attention to His word daily. Prov. 4:20,21. Many things and people will compete for your attention. **Who you give your attention to is who gives you direction.** What you give your attention to is what gives you direction. Your life is too precious to hand such power to someone other than God. When you are faced with a situation or someone, ask yourself, what is God saying about this? If you don't have a scripture in mind, listen to your heart. You will hear a word of direction and instruction. Follow it.

Two, build on principles based on God's word. These principles are in the Bible. Develop for yourself a study pattern which enables you to find promises and principles upon which you make decisions for living. Memorize these promises and principles. Confess them daily. When you are alone, speak them out loud to yourself. By so doing, you will be etching them on your subconscious. In the face of situations, they will pop out from you unconsciously.

Three, stay away from people and places that make a mockery of what you believe and practice. Keep them far from you. If they don't believe and practice it, they cannot be around your life. Friendship is not by force. It is by choice. You choose your friends. Don't let them impose themselves on you. You are going somewhere. If they are not going the same direction with you, there is no way you will end up where you intend to get to. If I am going to Lagos, I cannot join my childhood friend on his flight to Maiduguri just because he is my friend. I will keep my friendship and never get to my destination. Eventually, I will be miserable while he is happy. That is not what I want out of life. I want to be happy with my life.

As you do this, you will lose some friends. It is okay. When you succeed, they will come back. Failure is an orphan. Success has many friends.

"The poor is hated even of his own neighbour: but the rich hath many friends." Prov 14:20.

"Wealth maketh many friends; but the poor is separated from his neighbour." Prov 19:4.

Finally, protect your heart. Don't let unforgiveness, bitterness, strife, jealousy and envy lodge there. People will hurt you in order to manipulate or pollute you. Don't give them that power. They will say things and do things that will cause you to be bitter, don't allow them. Remember, you are going somewhere that is better than where you are today. Whatever it will cost you to get there, it is worth the sacrifice.

"Looking away [from all that will distract] to Jesus, Who is the Leader and the Source of our faith...He, for the joy [of obtaining the prize] that was set before Him, endured the cross,

despising and ignoring the shame, and is now seated at the right hand of the throne of God. Just think of Him Who endured from sinners such grievous opposition and bitter hostility against Himself [reckon up and consider it all in comparison with your trials], so that you may not grow weary or exhausted, losing heart and relaxing and fainting in your minds."
Heb. 12:2,3. (Amplified Version).

The power is in your mouth. You don't have to allow that Devil and his agents hold you hostage any more. I will never forget one day I was driving my daughter to school when suddenly she screamed, get out! I was surprised. I turned and asked her what. She said to me that the Devil was telling her something bad and she had to tell the Devil to get out. She was only four or five years then. She knew it was the Devil. She also knew to tell the Devil to get out. The power is in your mouth.

My marriage is getting better every day today because my wife and I are employing the power in our mouth for a glorious marriage. Sometimes my wife does things that really drive me crazy. The natural tendency is to retaliate. Do her something that will make her know that you are not to be taken for granted. When those evil thoughts start coming into my mind, I decide to say something different. I go out of my way to treat her right. It is my choice. I want to be happy. I must work towards what I want to see.

It is my marriage. If it works, I will enjoy it. I made my choice to enjoy every moment of the ride.

Don't shut your mouth and watch things go wrong in your world. If you don't like what you see, say something that you want to see. Speak until it looks like what you want to see. If you find weed on your corridor or yard, what do you do? Do you go about complaining that weeds are about taking over your house? I don't think so. Rather, you get your cutlass or mower and you go to work on your yard. If you want to see any kind of plant, you plant it. Water it daily and you will find it grows to beautify your world.

This is the same thing with life. If you have found the weeds of failure, unfavorable situations, excess fat, singleness, barrenness, joblessness, etc. Don't complain about it. Go to work on your garden. Cut them out. With your mouth, shout it out loud, I hate this. You can't stay here. You must leave. When you root out, don't forget to plant something different. Speak what you want to see. Water it every day with the words of your mouth.

"But the Lord said unto me, Say not, I am a child: for thou shalt go to all that I shall send thee, and whatsoever I command thee thou shalt speak.
Be not afraid of their faces: for I am with thee to deliver thee, saith the Lord.
Then the Lord put forth his hand, and touched my mouth. And the Lord said unto me, Behold, I have put my words in thy mouth.
See, I have this day set thee over the nations and over the kingdoms, to root out, and to pull down, and to destroy, and to throw down, to build, and to plant."

Jeremiah 1:7-10.

WHY I CHOSE JESUS CHRIST?

Someone asked me some years ago, *'Mike, why did you accept Jesus Christ?'* I could have been a Muslim, an atheist, a juju priest, etc. Why Jesus Christ?

My answer is simple: I accepted Jesus Christ for three reasons. One, I needed a Father. I needed to belong to Someone bigger than me, Someone who owned me because I came from Him. Two, I needed a Friend. I needed to partner with Someone who would always be there for me because He loves me just as I am. Three, I needed a Future. I needed Someone I could look up to everyday as a reason for living.

In my entire search, I found Jesus Christ to be everything I ever needed and would ever need. I accepted Him into my life and miracle of miracles; He came into my life and changed me. For three decades now, I still love Him. He is real and alive in me.

Today, you can make your choice. Choose you this day whom you will serve. Joshua 24:15. You have a choice: you can either RECEIVE CHRIST or you REJECT HIM. It is not by force. It is a choice you must make now.

If you choose Him, call on Him to come into your heart. He will. Rev. 3:20. Just say out loud: **"Jesus, I am a sinner. I accept Your sacrifice on the cross for me. Come into my heart and be my Lord and Master. Be my Father, Friend and Future. Change my life completely. I confess You as my Lord and Master from this day forward. Thank You Jesus for saving me today. Amen."**

Take a step to write to me or call on me. I will be glad to help you in your relationship with Jesus Christ - the reason for living!

FOR MORE INFORMATION

Send in your testimonies to let us know how this devotional has been a blessing to you.
Send in your prayer requests as well.
Stand with us to help us reach thirty million souls in fifty nations.
For more spiritual help, counseling and prayer ministration, contact:

**Bishop Michael O. Amamieye
Michael Amamieye Word Outreach,
International
a/k/a Aggressive Faith Ministries
Plot 13 Walter Akpana Lay Out off 394
Ikwerre Road, Mile 5 Rumueprikom, P. O.
Box 12378, Port Harcourt, Nigeria.
Hotlines: +234901800MAWO,
+2348050987377
WhatsApp: +2348036732188
U.S.A: +19162456157
www.aggressivefaith.org
E-mail: info@aggressivefaith.org**

ABOUT THE AUTHOR

Psalm 40:2,3 is a keynote to the life and ministry of Michael O. Amamieye. He was radically saved, healed and delivered from the power of darkness that endangered his youth. He is a living proof of God's matchless and abundant grace.

Since 1983, Brother Mike has been president, pastor and pioneer of several fellowships, churches and movements. He is instrumental in birthing many sons and daughters unto glory. He is a consecrated bishop with an oversight that reaches five continents.

In 1984, the Lord called Brother Mike to world evangelism with a mandate to ***take the gospel and miracle power of the risen Christ to the nations – impacting lives and destinies with the WORD!*** He is the President of **Michael Amamieye Word Outreach International** *also* *known as* **Aggressive Faith Ministries** with headquarters in the Garden City of Port Harcourt, Nigeria. He is the President of **Intensive Ministers Training School**. He is the Chairman of **Aggressive Faith Publishing Company**. Through this ministry, Brother Mike is determined to reach at least thirty million souls in at least fifty nations with the simple proclamation of the gospel of Christ with evidence that brings salvation, healing, deliverance, blessing and joy.

An evangelist by calling, he is a graduate of the **Billy Graham School of Evangelism**. He is a member of **Proclamation Evangelism Network** and an associate evangelist with the **Global Network of Evangelists** founded by the **Luis Palau Association**. He has been interviewed on **Decision Today** Radio broadcast and **Decision** magazine both of which are owned by the **Billy Graham Evangelistic Association.** He has also appeared on GODTV as well as several other networks around the world.

Bishop Mike is a member of the **International Communion of Charismatic Churches** founded by the late Archbishop Benson Idahosa and several others. He has been honored in a public ceremony where the Mayor of the city of East Cleveland, Ohio gave him the key to the city in 2003. **LEADS Africa** honored him as an icon of nation building in 2012. **The Voice** magazine in Holland honored him with the spiritual leadership award in 2014. In 2019, he was awarded an honorary doctorate degree by **Triune Biblical University** in New York. He is on high demand in crusades, conferences and conventions around the world.

He is the author of more than twenty books. He is a prolific and thought captivating writer with many of his works published in newsletters, magazines and newspapers around the world.

Bishop Mike is happily married to Princess Monivi, an ordained minister of the gospel and a health consultant. They are blessed with two biological children, Edwina Aleme and Mehetabel Favour as well as many others.

"They signaled to their partners in other boat to come and take hold with them. And they came and filled both the boats, so that they began to sink. " Luke 5:7. (Amplified Version).

Since the Lord gave me the vision of a massive harvest of souls through the mandate to reach 30 million souls for whom Christ died in at least 50 countries, I have not ceased to signal my partners *to come and take hold with me*.

Through our mass evangelistic crusades, we are seeing many become born again. It is amazing as God is giving us the gates of our enemies. We are seeing hardened criminals, cult leaders, gang leaders, etc, become born again.

This is possible because of the sacrifices of committed partners who have responded to our calls.

Now, it is your turn to respond to my signal. I want to give you an opportunity to fill your boat with miracles until it begins to sink.

Please check appropriate boxes:

☐ **I WANT TO BECOME A MONTHLY PARTNER.** I am expecting my partner information packet with more details. My offering is enclosed to start my partnership. I am willing to commit monthly: ☐ **$15** ☐ **$20** ☐ **$25** ☐ **$50** ☐ **$100**

☐ **I WANT TO HELP SPONSOR A CRUSADE.** Enclosed is my special one-time gift of: ☐ **$1000** ☐ **$2000** ☐ **$3000** ☐ **$__________**

Tear this form and send to us with your prayer requests.
Use the address you find in this book.